ANIMAL SWIMMING AND DIVING

Isabel Thomas

capstone

Edited by Linda Staniford
Designed by Steve Mead
Picture research by Kelly Garvin
Production by Victoria Fitzgerald
Originated by Capstone Global Library Ltd
Printed and bound in China

19 18 17 16 15
10 9 8 7 6 5 4 3 2 1

Library of Congress Cataloging-in-Publication Data
Cataloging-in-publication information is on file with the Library of Congress.
Written by Isabel Thomas
ISBN 978-1-4109-8092-2 (hardcover)
ISBN 978-1-4109-8100-4 (eBook PDF)

Acknowledgments
The author and publisher are grateful to the following for permission to reproduce copyright material:
Getty Images: Adam Pretty, 10, Francois Xavier Marit/AFP, 4; Minden Pictures: Hiroya Minakuchi, 9, Pete Oxford, 12, 13; Nature Picture Library: Charlie Hamilton James, 25, Doc White, 24, Espen Bergersen, 19, Stephen Dalton, 7, Tim Laman, 23; Newscom: Aly Song/Rueters, 14, Dennis M.Sabangan/EPA, 22, Erich Schlegel/MCT, 6, George Karbus Photography Culture, 5, Mark Reis/KRT, 18, Pool/Rueters, 27, Saul Gonor/Evolve/Photoshot, 16; Seapics.com: James D. Watt, 21, Michael Patrick O'Neill, 8; Shutterstock: Alexius Sutandio, 17, David Carbo, cover, (top left), Eric Isselee, cover (bottom right), Hiroshi Sato, 11, Kotomiti Okuma, cover (bottom left), Leonardo Gonzalez, 20, Neirfy, cover, (top right), Sylvie Bouchard, 15, 31

Artistic Elements: kavalenkava volha, La Gorda, Nikiteev_Konstantin, PinkPueblo, Potapov Alexander, Stockobaza, yyang.

We would like to thank Michael Bright for his help in the preparation of this book.

007494CTPSS16

Key₀

 Mammals

 Birds

 Fish

 Reptiles and Amphibians

 Invertebrates

CONTENTS

Some words are shown in bold, **like this**. You can find out what they mean by looking in the glossary.

LET THE GAMES BEGIN!

The world's best athletes come together every four years to compete at the Olympic Games. Swimming events test their skill, strength, and speed in the water. Diving events are a display of coordination and control as divers perform amazing routines.

Most swimming and diving events take place in a 164-foot- (50-meter-) long swimming pool.

You don't have to head to an Olympic swimming pool to see amazing speed and skill in the water. In rivers and oceans, you'll find animals that can beat the best human swimmers. Speedy swimming and diving skills are **adaptations** that help these animals to **survive**. Let's find out which animal swimmers and divers deserve a medal at the Animalympics!

FREESTYLE

The 50-meter freestyle is the fastest Olympic swimming race. Swimmers pull their arms through the water and kick their legs up and down to zoom down one length of the pool in as little as 21 seconds. How does this compare to animals that swim in a similar way?

The fastest human swimmers can cover 7.5 feet (2.3 meters) every second.

Goggles protect eyes and help swimmers see underwater.

Whirligig beetle

Whirligig beetles are the champion insect swimmers. Like Olympic swimmers, they can turn very quickly in the water. Their back legs have bristles that pop out like paddles for each **stroke**.

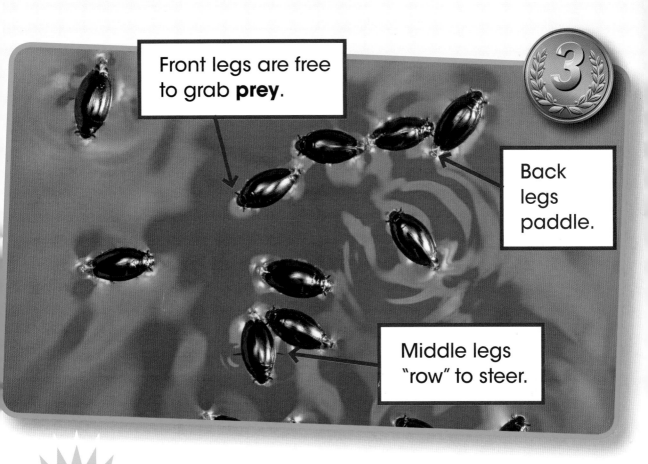

Front legs are free to grab **prey**.

Back legs paddle.

Middle legs "row" to steer.

These beetles dive under the surface to escape **predators**.

Leatherback turtle

Leatherback turtles swim by paddling their flippers. They are the speediest reptile swimmers, traveling at 9.2 feet (2.8 meters) per second. This means a leatherback turtle would beat the best Olympic freestyle swimmers by about three seconds!

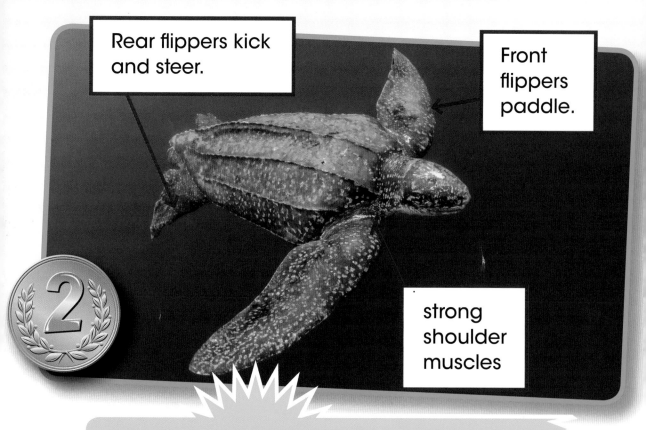

Rear flippers kick and steer.

Front flippers paddle.

strong shoulder muscles

Turtles are adapted to swim and dive long distances to hunt for **prey** and hide from **predators**.

wings adapted for paddling

 Gentoo penguin

The speediest penguins can zoom through water four times faster than humans, at 22.4 miles (36 kilometers) per hour! Penguins can boost their speed by squeezing air bubbles out of their feathers. The air bubbles help the penguins to slip through the water easily.

Like humans, Gentoo penguins swim by paddling.

BUTTERFLY

In butterfly races, swimmers drag both arms through the water at the same time. Their legs also move up and down together in a "dolphin kick." Olympic swimmers can butterfly 164 feet (50 meters) in less than 22.5 seconds.

lane

lane line

🐻 Dolphin

Most fish, and **marine mammals** such as dolphins and whales, swim in a similar way. Instead of paddling with arms, legs, or flippers, they flap their tails up and down, or from side to side. Bottlenose dolphins can flap their tails up and down 180 times a minute!

Bottlenose dolphins can speed along more than four times faster than humans, at up to 22 miles (35 kilometers) per hour!

Marine iguanas

Marine iguanas are the only lizards to find their food at sea, so they are adapted to swim differently than other lizards. Like butterfly swimmers, they move through the water using **undulations**, at up to 1.9 miles (3 kilometers) per hour.

flattened tail, like a fish

legs tucked in

Tail and body move from side to side.

Marine iguanas use their swimming skills to feed on **algae** growing on underwater rocks.

 # Sailfish

Sailfish and swordfish are the speediest animals in the sea. By moving their tails and bodies from side to side, these fish can reach speeds of over 62 miles (100 kilometers) per hour in short bursts.

When a sailfish attacks **prey**, it folds its fins back against its body for a burst of speed.

Sailfish knock out prey with their noses.

Fins fold back.

MARATHON

Olympic marathon swimmers battle 6.2 miles (10 kilometers) of open water in a sea, river, lake, or canal. The marathon distance is the same as 200 lengths of a normal Olympic pool. Top distance swimmers have done this in just under two hours.

 Polar bear

Polar bears paddle with their front paws. They aren't fast, but they are great long-distance swimmers. One polar bear was tracked swimming for nine days without stopping. She covered 426 miles (685 kilometers)—that's almost 70 Olympic swimming marathon courses!

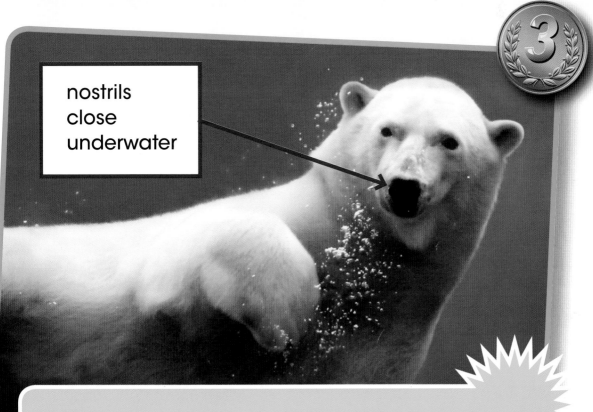

nostrils close underwater

When the Arctic sea ice melts in summer, polar bears swim long distances to reach land.

Humpback whale

Humpback whales feed near the North and South poles, but **migrate** to warmer oceans every year to breed. They travel around 3,000 miles (5,000 kilometers) on average. The longest humpback journey on record was 6,090 miles (9,800 kilometers), from Brazil to Madagascar.

long flippers

huge tail **fluke**

Great white shark

Gold for the fastest swimming in the marathon event goes to the great white shark. In 2004, a female great white made a 12,400-mile (20,000-kilometer) journey from Africa to Australia and back in just nine months.

Scientists have proven that a shark's rough skin helps it to slip through the water more easily, helping it to use less energy as it swims.

SYNCHRONIZED SWIMMING

Synchronized swimming is like underwater gymnastics. Swimmers spin, twist, float, dive, and lift each other to make shapes and patterns with their bodies. Speakers blast music underwater to help the swimmers keep time.

Whales and dolphins

Whales and dolphins often swim and surface together in perfect harmony. Swimming close together helps the whales respond quickly to danger.

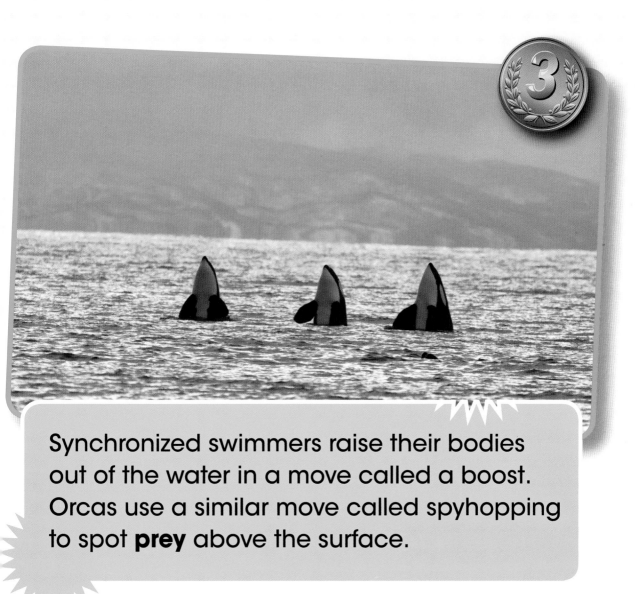

Synchronized swimmers raise their bodies out of the water in a move called a boost. Orcas use a similar move called spyhopping to spot **prey** above the surface.

Schools of fish

Schools are enormous groups of fish swimming together. Each fish matches its movements to those of its nearest neighbor, so the whole school turns, darts, and dives together.

Synchronized swimming helps fish to avoid crashing into each other. It also helps fish blend into the crowd, so that they are less likely to be snapped up by a predator.

 Pilotfish

Pilotfish have the same synchronized swimming skills as other schooling fish. But they get extra points for creativity! Pilotfish swim under sharks to save energy. They also get to nibble scraps of the **predator's** food.

shark

pilotfish

DIVING

Divers leap into the water from platforms and springboards. They perform somersaults, twists, tucks, and pikes before gliding into the water as smoothly as possible.

Proboscis monkey

Proboscis monkeys spend their days high up in trees, chomping leaves. If a **predator** creeps up on them, the monkeys have an escape route. They are able to dive into the nearest stream.

Proboscis monkeys have been seen diving from branches up to 52.5 feet (16 meters) tall—20 feet (6 meters) higher than the Olympic diving platform!

Elephant seal

When Olympic divers plunge into a pool, they travel about 16 feet (5 meters) underwater. Elephant seals can keep going until they are nearly 5,000 feet (more than 1,500 meters) deep! They hold their breath for up to two hours, as they hunt for squid and other **prey** hiding in the ocean depths.

Elephant seals have three to four times more blood than a land mammal of the same size.

Kingfisher

Kingfishers dive into water headfirst to grab their fish prey. Olympic divers earn extra points for entering the water without a splash. This is important for kingfishers, too. If they made a big splash, fish would feel the ripples in time to dart to safety.

wings folded in for high speed

long, pointed beak

AMAZING ADAPTATIONS

Animals don't swim or dive well as a sport. The body features that make animals good at swimming and diving are **adaptations** that help them to **survive**. These features help animals to find food, attract mates, care for their young, or avoid getting eaten. They are more likely to be passed on to the next **generation**.

Watching record-breaking animal swimmers also helps scientists find out how animal bodies work. This information is used in amazing ways, such as designing boats and submarines that can move through the water using as little energy as possible.

Scientists copied features of a shark's skin to create a swimsuit that helps swimmers move through the water more quickly.

MEDAL TABLE

It's time for the Animalympic medal ceremony! The animal kingdom is divided into groups. Animals with similar features belong to the same class. Which class will take home the most medals for swimming and diving?

 ## Mammals

Mammals are warm-blooded animals with hair or fur that feed milk to their young. Marine mammals live in the water all the time, but many land mammals are also great swimmers.

 ## Reptiles and Amphibians

Reptiles and amphibians are cold-blooded animals. Adult amphibians can't breathe underwater, but amphibians have webbed feet, and spend part of their lives living underwater.

 ## Birds

Birds have feathers, wings, and a beak. Many hunt at sea, but they can't spend long underwater.

 ## Invertebrates

This group includes all animals without a backbone, such as insects, spiders, and snails. They are found in all habitats, including the deepest oceans.

 ## Fish

Fish live in saltwater or freshwater. They have fins for swimming and gills to breathe underwater.

RESULTS

EVENT	3 BRONZE	2 SILVER	1 GOLD
FREESTYLE	Whirligig beetle	Leatherback turtle	Gentoo penguin
BUTTERFLY	Dolphin	Marine iguana	Sailfish
MARATHON	Polar bear	Humpback whale	Great white shark
SYNCHRONIZED SWIMMING	Whales and dolphins	Schools of fish	Pilotfish
DIVING	Proboscis monkey	Elephant seal	Kingfisher

ANIMAL	RANK	GOLD	SILVER	BRONZE
Fish	1	🥇🥇🥇	🥈	
Birds	2	🥇🥇		
Mammals	3		🥈🥈	🥉🥉🥉🥉
Reptiles and amphibians	4		🥈🥈	
Invertebrates	5			🥉

29

GLOSSARY

adaptation changes to the body, workings, or behavior of a living thing that make it better suited to its habitat

algae simple plant-like living things that live in the sea and freshwater

fluke one of the forking "arms" of a whale's tail

generation group of living things that were born, or are living, at the same time

marine mammal mammal that lives, or spends most of its time, in the sea

migrate move from one place to another when the seasons change

predator animal that hunts and kills other animals for food

prey animal that is hunted and killed by another animal for food

stroke combination of arm and leg movements in swimming

survive stay alive

undulation up and down or side-to-side movements of a tail or body

FIND OUT MORE

Books

de la Bédoyère, Camilla. *Could a Whale Swim to the Moon?*
   Irvine, Calif.: QEB, 2015.

Morey, Allan. *Swimming and Diving* (Summer Olympic
   Sports). Mankato, Minn.: Amicus, 2016.

Murphy, Julie. *Amazing Animal Adaptations* series.
   Mankato, Minn.: Capstone, 2012.

Internet sites

Facthound offers a safe, fun way to find Internet
sites related to this book. All of the sites on
Facthound have been researched by our staff.

Here's all you do:
Visit www.facthound.com
Type in this code: 9781410980922

INDEX